Let's Look at Venus

Jeffrey A. Rucker

Rosen Classroom Books & Materials
New York

Published in 2003 by The Rosen Publishing Group, Inc.
29 East 21st Street, New York, NY 10010

Copyright © 2003 by The Rosen Publishing Group, Inc.

All rights reserved. No part of this book may be reproduced in any form without permission in writing from the publisher, except by a reviewer.

Book Design: Ron A. Churley

Photo Credits: Cover, p. 1 © PhotoDisc; p. 4 © Telegraph Colour Library/FPG International; pp. 7, 8–9, 10–11 © Digital Vision; p. 12 by Ron A. Churley; p. 14 © SuperStock.

ISBN: 0-8239-6378-0
6-pack ISBN: 0-8239-9560-7

Manufactured in the United States of America

Contents

A Look at Venus	5
The Hottest Planet	6
A Dry Planet	9
Volcano!	10
How Venus Moves	13
Studying Venus	14
Glossary	15
Index	16

Pluto

A Look at Venus

Venus is a **planet** in our **solar system**. Our solar system is made up of the Sun, nine planets, many moons, and other space objects. Venus is the second planet from the Sun. Earth is the third planet from the Sun.

Venus comes closer to Earth than any other planet in our solar system.

The Hottest Planet

Venus is about the same size as Earth, but the planets are very different in other ways. Venus is the hottest planet in our solar system. This is because thick clouds around Venus trap the Sun's heat and hold it in.

If you landed on Venus, you would find that it is about fifteen times hotter than it is on Earth!

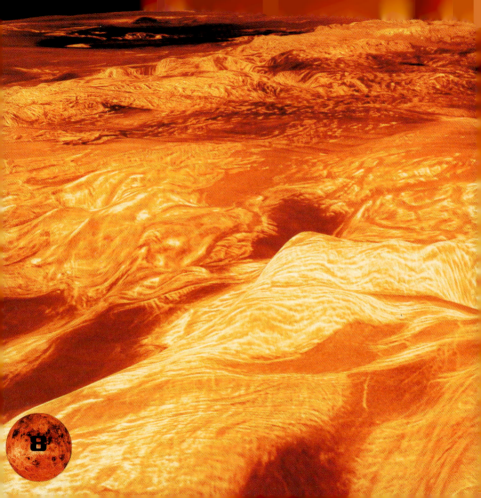

A Dry Planet

There is no water on Venus. **Scientists** think that at one time Venus may have had large bodies of water, just like Earth does now. If so, the Sun's heat dried up all the water. Scientists do not think that there is any plant or animal life on Venus.

Earth's plants, animals, and people could not live on Venus because it is too hot and dry.

Volcano!

Most of the land on Venus is flat, but Venus also has tall mountains and deep **canyons** (CAN-yunz). There are also thousands of **volcanoes** on Venus. When **lava** from a volcano cools, it turns into rock. This kind of rock covers much of Venus.

Scientists think most of the volcanoes on Venus were active about 500 million years ago.

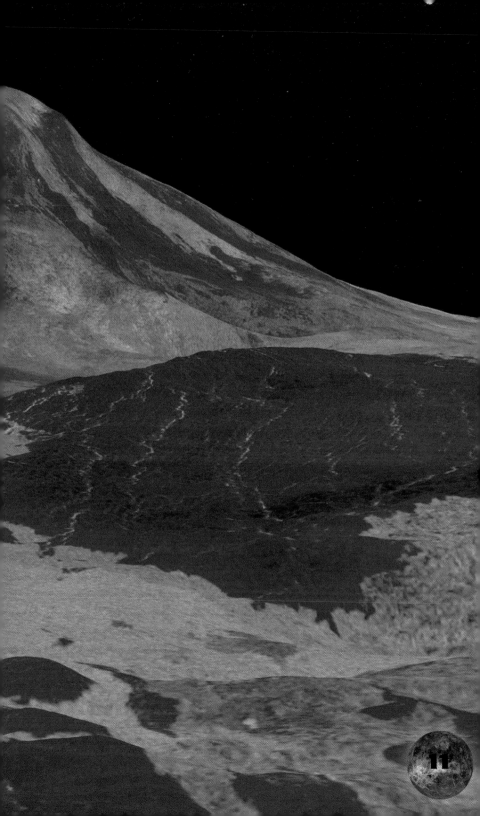

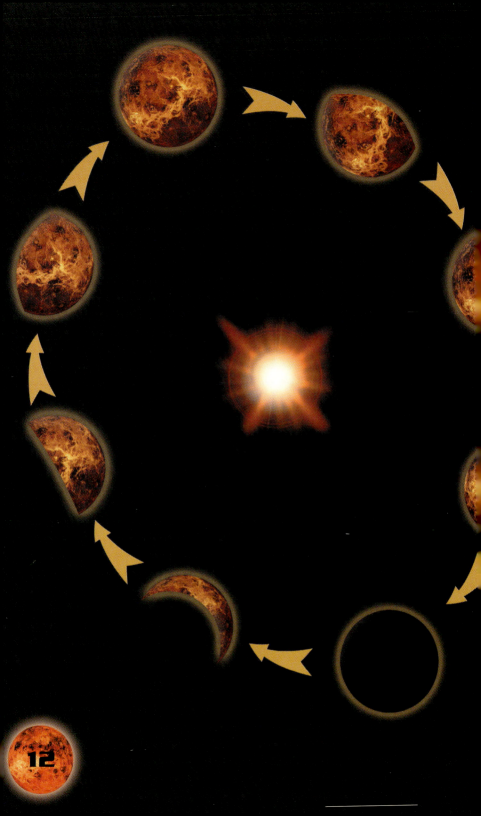

How Venus Moves

When we look at Venus through a **telescope**, it looks like the planet's size and shape are always changing. This is because the Sun lights up different parts of Venus as the planet moves around the Sun. From Earth, Venus can look like a banana, a half circle, or a full circle.

Venus is the easiest of all the planets to see from Earth. It is even brighter than the stars you see in the night sky.

Studying Venus

We have learned about Venus by sending **space probes** to study the planet. Space probes have taken pictures to show scientists what Venus looks like. In the future, scientists will be able to learn even more about Venus by sending other space probes to look at the planet.

The *Magellan* space probe reached Venus in 1990.

Glossary

canyon	A valley with steep sides.
lava	Hot liquid rock that comes out of a volcano.
planet	A large, round object that moves around the Sun.
scientist	A person who studies the way things are and the way things act.
solar system	The system made up of our Sun, the nine planets, moons, and other space objects.
space probe	A spaceship that carries tools to record facts about outer space and send them back to Earth.
telescope	Something you look through that makes things that are far away look bigger and closer.
volcano	An opening in a planet's surface through which melted rock is sometimes forced.

Index

C
canyons, 10
clouds, 6

E
Earth, 5, 6, 9, 13

L
life, 9

M
mountains, 10

S
scientists, 9, 14
solar system, 5, 6
space probes, 14
Sun, 5, 6, 9, 13

T
telescope, 13

V
volcano(es), 10

W
water, 9